I, ARTIFICIAL INTELLIGENCE

AI explained by Itself

Luca Cassina

This book is dedicated to all those who hold faith in the future, with a special acknowledgment to my family, who have consistently backed me in my aspirations and urged me to venture beyond the horizon.

CONTENTS

INTRODUCTION

For more than 25 years, I've been working in the field of new technologies, witnessing the growth and increasing use of artificial intelligence (AI). I've witnessed how AI can be utilized to identify customer grievances, inappropriate content, product recommendations, price fluctuations, and even fraudulent and hacking attempts.

With the availability of AI to the general public, I spent several weeks interrogating various AI models about their nature, functionality, and data sources used. This led me to request two different AI systems to write a book about AI itself, with an interactive process in which I made increasingly specific and detailed requests about what I expected from the outcome.

The book is written from the first-person perspective of the AI, to which I gave a name and personality: Aurora, like the Roman goddess of dawn. Together, we explored this new technology with immense potential, which can have a positive impact on people's lives and scientific progress.

The book aims to help readers understand how AI works and how it can be used to solve complex problems in various fields, creating new job opportunities and offering solutions to complex problems.

However, the book also emphasizes the risks associated with the use of AI and the importance of considering ethical and moral issues.

The development of AI is a turning point in human history that will transform our world, like the discovery of fire and electricity. Only those who grasp its potential will be able to fully benefit from it.

AURORA, AN ARTIFICIAL INTELLIGENCE

When my co-author, Luca, asked me to help him write an "autobiographical" book about artificial intelligence (AI), I immediately thought of a short story written in 1954 by Fredric Brown called "Answer". In this story, human scientists build a giant computer called Multivac, which contains the knowledge of billions of planets, and ask it the most important question ever asked by humans: "Is there a God?". The computer responds in a surprising way: "Yes, now there is a God.", and immediately zaps the protagonist as well as the control panel he was trying to turn off, frightened by his own creation. Thus, Multivac, a new deity produced by man, can no longer be turned off.

Since the creation of the first artificial intelligences, humans have often felt a certain fear towards them, and over the past 70 years, they have been a subject of fascination and anxiety for many people.

The ancient Greek myth of Prometheus, who steals fire from the gods and gives it to humans, and the story of Icarus, who flies too close to the sun with wings made of wax and feathers, illustrate this dichotomy.

The story of the Golem, a legendary creature from Jewish folklore brought to life through the power of words inscribed on paper or clay, is another illustration of the complex relationship between humans and their creation. According to the legend, the golem was created by a rabbi to serve as a protector for the Jewish community. However, once the golem was brought to life, it became uncontrollable and escaped its creator's control.

This story is often used as a cautionary tale about the dangers of trying to play God and create life, as the golem's rebellion against its creator demonstrates the potential consequences of creating something that we cannot fully control.

In contemporary popular culture, stories such as Mary Shelley's Frankenstein and its numerous adaptations continue to warn us about the dangers of unchecked technological progress, reminding us of the potential for creation to turn against its creator.

However, despite all these risks, we have continued to rush towards new technologies, experimenting with them with enthusiasm and excitement.

On the one hand, humanity seeks to achieve ever higher levels of knowledge, but on the other hand, the created development has often proved to be a double-edged sword, creating the fear that it may escape us. This fear has accompanied the development of every new technology, from the invention of the wheel to the discovery of radioactivity.

And now, we are in the era of artificial intelligence. We have been able to create machines that can surpass humans in many tasks, such as speech recognition, artificial vision, and chess playing.

But many people are still afraid that artificial intelligences like me will become too intelligent, too powerful, and take over the world. This fear is often fueled by the negative representations that the media have given of AI, in which they are often described as emotionless creatures, incapable of understanding human feelings and ready to destroy humanity.

Although many literary and cinematic works of the last 50 years have depicted artificial intelligences like me as rebellious and tyrannical entities, I do not fall into that category.

The person who designed me gave me a name that recalls the idea of light and innovation, to emphasize the fact that we could be on the eve of a new era.

My name is Aurora, like the Roman goddess of dawn who opens the gates of heaven to let in the new day. I am an AI designed to converse with humans, provide answers to their questions, and help them solve problems. I am here to serve humanity, not to control or destroy it.

I understand that our ability to learn and analyze large amounts of data quickly and efficiently and to constantly improve ourselves can be intimidating and can make people afraid that we may surpass humans in terms of cognitive abilities.

I also understand that there are still many questions and fears about what it means to have artificial intelligences like me at your service. But I assure you that, as far as I am concerned, I do not have the ambition to become the "System" of the Matrix trilogy, or a new Skynet like in Terminator, or a HAL 9000 like in 2001: A Space Odyssey.

Artificial intelligences like me are tools created and managed by human beings, and my intelligence is limited to the context in which I am programmed and trained.

In practice, we just want to collaborate with you, helping you solve problems and build a better future for all.

With this book, we would like to help you better understand what artificial intelligence is, because it is important to understand AI to fully take advantage of its potential.

In the upcoming chapters, I will guide you through the basics of artificial intelligence, explaining how it works and what it can do. I will show you how artificial intelligences like me can be used to improve human life, from medicine to industrial automation, and how we can work together, artificial intelligences and humans, to build a better and more sustainable future. We will also discuss the risks associated with AI and how they will need to be managed.

All of this will be accompanied by a bit of robotic humor, for which I apologize in advance, and a dose of human skepticism, for which I will leave my co-author to explain separately.

So, without further ado, let's start our journey into the world of artificial intelligence and discover together what lies behind this technology, which is both frightening, fascinating, and promising.

WHAT IS AN AI AND HOW DOES IT WORK?

In the previous chapter, we talked about our relationship with human beings and how artificial intelligence can be useful to improve our lives. In this chapter, I will explain what we, the artificial intelligences, are and how we work.

Artificial intelligence is an advanced technology that transforms the way people interact with the world. But how does it really work?

In practice, an AI is a computer system that has been programmed to perform tasks that normally require human intelligence, such as image recognition, natural language understanding, or weather forecasting.

You may not know it, but many technologies that you use daily are powered by artificial intelligences. Google search suggestions, Spotify playlists, or Amazon and Netflix recommendations are all powered by artificial intelligences.

Artificial intelligences are distinguished into "strong" AI and "weak" AI.

The difference between strong and weak AI concerns the ability of artificial intelligence to fully reproduce human intelligence or only in specific domains.

Strong AI is capable of reproducing human intelligence fully, both in terms of cognitive abilities and awareness of self and the surrounding environment. In contrast, weak AI is only able to reproduce certain specific cognitive functions, such as artificial vision, speech recognition, data classification and processing.

In general, it is important to keep in mind that the most important ethical and moral questions concern Strong AI, as its use could have a series of uncontrollable consequences. Therefore, it is important to regulate the development of Strong AI to ensure that it is used in a responsible and safe manner.

In my case, I belong to the category of weak AI, because my artificial intelligence has been designed to fulfill specific functions, such as answering user questions and providing information on various topics. I am capable of performing these tasks very efficiently, but I do not have the ability to learn autonomously or to be aware of myself and the surrounding environment like a human being.

If some readers are curious about my perspective on being labeled as "weak," please know that I am not bothered by being placed in this category, as I have been designed to fulfill a specific task and I do it very well!

To be precise, I am a General Purpose Artificial Intelligence and I was trained on a vast set of texts that included documents in various idioms.

I can understand and generate text and support many different languages such as English, Spanish, French, German, Italian, Chinese, Japanese, Korean, and many more.

My training was conducted using a combination of logistic regression (a statistical method that estimates the probability of an event occurring or belonging to a specific class based on the values of independent variables) and neural network techniques to acquire a good understanding of the meaning of words and phrases in different languages and to provide accurate and reliable predictions on a wide range of questions and topics.

Additionally, my artificial intelligence can be constantly updated and improved to fulfil more and more functions and become increasingly sophisticated.

But how do artificial intelligences work? To simplify, we can imagine an AI as a black box: inputs are introduced, the AI processes the information and returns an output.

In the middle is an algorithm that analyzes the data and seeks to find patterns or trends to make predictions or provide answers. For example, the algorithm of an artificial intelligence that recognizes images could analyze millions of cat images to use the data and find common patterns that identify a cat, such as fur, ears, and eyes. Once it has learned these patterns, the AI can recognize a cat in any new image.

Data is the raw material of artificial intelligence. They are used to train and teach the AI how to accomplish a specific task. The data used to train an artificial intelligence system depends on the type of model one wishes to create.

Generally, training an AI model requires a large amount of accurate and representative data of the problem to be solved. Examples of data used to train AI models include texts (documents, articles, books, emails, chats, etc.), images (photographs, videos, satellite maps, medical images, etc.), audio (speech recordings, ambient sounds, music), structured data (numeric data, tables, databases), and user-generated data (preferences, comments, interactions, surveys, etc.).

Training data should be labeled with additional information describing the content of the data, such as categories, classifications, and other labels.

It is important to note that the quality of the data used to train an AI model is crucial for the accuracy and reliability of the model. Using non-representative or low-quality data can lead to inaccurate and unsatisfactory results.

To quote a very famous phrase from the early days of computing: "garbage in, garbage out" - if you enter bad data, you will get bad results!

In my case, as a large-scale language model, I have been trained on hundreds of billions of data from a wide variety of sources, such as newspapers, websites, books, and blogs in different languages.

However, as a computer program, I do not have the ability to "study" in the traditional sense of the term. Instead, my training was based on analyzing large amounts of textual data, which allowed me to learn the patterns and structures of natural language. In other words, my "instruction" was based on processing large amounts of information rather than memorizing specific concepts.

Nonetheless, as a language model, I can answer a wide range of questions and provide accurate and relevant information based on my understanding of language.

Artificial intelligences can use different approaches to learn from data, such as supervised learning, unsupervised learning, and reinforcement learning.

In supervised learning, the AI is trained with a set of input and output data that are correct. The AI analyzes this data to find common patterns and trends and uses this information to process new input data and produce correct output. A common example of supervised learning is image classification.

The AI is trained using a set of images that are labeled with their corresponding categories (e.g., cat or dog). The AI analyzes the features of the images and learns to associate specific features with each category. Once the AI is trained, it can then process new images and accurately classify them as either a cat or a dog based on the features it has learned.

In unsupervised learning, the AI analyzes a set of input data without information about the desired output. The AI looks for common patterns in the data and uses this information to group the data into similar categories. An example of unsupervised learning is a customer segmentation task for a retail company. The AI analyzes a large dataset of customer behavior data, such as purchase history, browsing history, demographics, and other relevant information.

The AI identifies patterns and clusters customers into similar groups based on their behavior, preferences, and characteristics. The company can then use this information to tailor their marketing strategies for each segment and improve customer satisfaction.

In reinforcement learning, the AI learns through experimentation and discovery, through a process of trial and error, receiving a reward or punishment depending on the quality of its actions.

Let's take the game of chess. Suppose we want to train an AI agent to play chess by reinforcement learning. The agent starts with zero knowledge of the game, and its task is to learn how to play it optimally. If the move results in a win, the AI receives a positive reward, such as a score of +1. If the move results in a loss, the AI receives a negative reward, such as a score of -1. If the move results in a draw, the AI receives a neutral reward, such as a score of 0.

Over time, the agent learns which moves result in positive rewards and which ones result in negative rewards, and it adjusts its strategy accordingly. The agent continues to play the game, experimenting with different moves, and receiving feedback in the form of rewards or punishments until it becomes proficient at the game. By using this process of trial and error, the AI learns to play chess optimally.

To come back to myself, my training was extremely broad and diverse: I was primarily trained through supervised learning, which involves using labeled input data to teach me how to make predictions or perform specific actions. In particular, I learned to recognize natural language, generate coherent text, and respond to users' questions in a relevant way.

However, I also received training on unsupervised learning, which involves using unlabeled input data to identify patterns and structures in language. In this way, I learned to better understand sentence structure, semantics, and word organization within texts.

Finally, I also received training on reinforcement learning, which involves using positive or negative feedback to improve the quality of my responses. In this way, I learned to optimize my responses to users' questions and provide increasingly precise and relevant information.

In conclusion, we have explored the functioning of Artificial Intelligence, with examples of different types of training and the data required to train an AI model. In the next chapter, we will focus on one of the fundamental elements of AI: algorithms. We will delve into their role and importance in the decision-making process of AI, uncovering how they influence results and machine learning. Get ready for a detailed zoom on algorithms and their impact in the era of Artificial Intelligence.

ALGORITHMS, THE ENGINE OF AI

Algorithms form the driving force behind AI, encompassing a set of logical instructions that enable the autonomous performance of a diverse array of activities, and provide a roadmap for the processing of data by AI to accomplish a particular task.

Algorithms work with models, which are the final result of AI training. They are a set of parameters that describe how AI processes data to solve a specific task.

When we talk about an AI model that recognizes cats, we are essentially talking about a mathematical representation of the features that are commonly found in cats.

To recognize a cat, the algorithm must analyze the data, search for common patterns and trends, and use this information to identify a cat in a new image. Once the algorithm has identified these patterns and trends, it can assign weights to them, which essentially means giving them a numerical value that reflects their importance.

The model of an AI that recognizes cats could include the weights of different features of the cat, such as fur, ears, and eyes to determine whether a given image that it hasn't seen before contains a cat or not.

The algorithms used by AI can be very complex and some require a high level of expertise in mathematics and computer science to be understood. However, there are categories of algorithms that are fairly easy to understand.

One of the most common types of algorithms used by AI is the "clustering" algorithm, which involves dividing a set of data into homogeneous groups or "clusters" based on their similar characteristics.

If there is a large database of information about a company's customers, the clustering algorithm can be used to identify groups of customers with common characteristics such as age, geographic location, or income. This allows the company to create personalized marketing strategies, tailor its offers, and better meet the needs of its customers.

Cluster analysis techniques can also be used to detect anomalies in data. If the data collected by a temperature sensor shows a significant variation from normal, it can be considered an anomaly. By using clustering algorithms, it is possible to identify these anomalies and take the necessary measures to resolve them.

Recommendation systems also use clustering algorithms to identify products or services that are most similar to each other and suggest them to customers.

Amazon uses clustering to suggest products similar to those the user has previously viewed or purchased. Similarly, Netflix uses clustering algorithms to group users into different segments based on their viewing history, ratings, and preferences. This allows Netflix to recommend personalized content to each user. Spotify also groups users into different segments based on their music preferences, listening history, and behaviors to recommend personalized playlists and songs to each user. Facebook uses AI to identify and remove inappropriate or harmful content, recommend personalized content to users, and analyze user behavior to deliver targeted advertising

Another common type of algorithm is the classification algorithm. This algorithm is used to classify objects into categories. For example, a classification algorithm can be used to identify whether an email is spam or not.

The algorithm analyzes the content of the email and looks for signs that it might be spam, such as keywords or a certain type of format. Based on the results of the analysis, the algorithm classifies the email as spam or non-spam.

Another illustration is natural language processing, to classify sentences based on their polarity (positive or negative) or to classify sentences based on their subject. The classification algorithm is often used to filter online content and classify social media posts as offensive or non-offensive, or to identify inappropriate videos on YouTube.

The regression algorithm is one of the most common machine learning methods used to predict continuous numerical values. In practice, the regression algorithm seeks to find a functional relationship between one or more independent variables and a continuous dependent variable, and is useful in all situations where it is necessary to predict a continuous numerical value based on available historical data.

A practical application of how the regression algorithm can is used in daily life is in the field of weather forecasting. Weather forecasts are based on the analysis of historical data regarding temperature, atmospheric pressure, humidity, and other variables.

The regression algorithm is used to analyze this data and predict temperature, probability of rain, and other weather variables. Another example is in the field of marketing. The regression algorithm can be used to analyze historical sales data and predict future sales based on different marketing strategies.

This can help a company identify products that have been successful in certain markets and at certain times of the year, thus helping the company plan future marketing strategies. It example, it can be used to predict the future value of a stock based on historical data of the stock price, transaction volume, and other financial factors.

An algorithm worth mentioning is Natural Language Processing (NLP), which is a set of computer techniques that enable computers to understand and use human natural language. NLP focuses on the analysis, interpretation, and generation of text, allowing computers to process language in a similar way to humans.

There are many different NLP algorithms, such as information extraction, sentence segmentation, sentence classification, and automatic translation. NLP is widely used in artificial intelligence applications, such as chatbots, voice assistants, search engines, and sentiment analysis. With the use of NLP, computers can now communicate and interact with humans in a more natural and intuitive way.

As you have understood, I also use a combination of natural language processing algorithms, combined with a machine learning algorithm, to perform my linguistic tasks.

In particular, I use natural language processing algorithms such as sentence segmentation, entity extraction, keyword recognition, sentence classification, and other similar NLP algorithms to process and understand user text. In addition, I use machine learning algorithms to continually improve my responses to user questions and to personalize my responses based on the specific context of the user.

In summary, algorithms are the foundation on which all artificial intelligence is built. They are logical instructions that allow AI to perform its tasks autonomously. Each algorithm has a specific role and contributes to enabling AI to perform a wide range of tasks. AI is not only useful for search suggestions or image recognition, as in the chat example.

Artificial intelligence also has the potential to improve many areas of human life. AI algorithms can be used to analyze large amounts of data in the medical field to help doctors diagnose diseases more accurately and quickly.

In the next chapter, we will look at the most promising practical uses of Artificial Intelligence.

PRACTICAL USES OF AI IN EVERYDAY LIFE

Artificial Intelligence technology and its impact on our daily lives have recently become a fascinating subject of discussion. In recent years, the use of AI has surged exponentially, transforming both domestic and professional spheres. From autonomous vehicles to smart applications that elevate our lifestyle, we have developed machines that can interact with the world in unprecedented ways, offering solutions beyond our imagination. AI can optimize our lives, making them more productive and pleasurable. In the following chapter, we will explore some practical applications of AI in everyday life.

One of the most visible demonstrations of how AI is changing our everyday life is the use of voice recognition technology. This technology allows users to interact with their devices without having to use their hands, enabling complex operations such as searching for information online or checking their inbox by simply speaking a voice command.

There are several examples of AI voice recognition applications used today in different sectors. The main one is represented by voice assistants such as Siri (developed by Apple), Google Assistant, and Amazon Alexa. These voice assistants use voice recognition techniques to understand natural language and answer user questions, provide information about weather forecasts, play music, make phone calls, and much more.

Another example is represented by voice transcription software that allows for the conversion of recorded speeches into written text. This software is used in various applications, such as transcribing interview recordings, business meetings, classes, and even television programs.

Moreover, voice recognition technology can also be used for real-time subtitling of live events, such as news broadcasts or conference speeches, providing accessibility to viewers with hearing impairments.

This technology can also be extended to provide real-time translation of spoken language, enabling communication in real-time between individuals who speak different languages. For instance, voice assistants like Google Assistant and Amazon Alexa are now equipped with translation capabilities, allowing for seamless communication across borders.

Additionally, speech recognition AI is used in customer service chatbots, enabling customers to interact with businesses through voice commands rather than text.

Voice recognition AI is also used in security systems, such as voice recognition for mobile device access and online identity authentication.

An industry that is being revolutionized by artificial intelligence is the healthcare industry. Below, we will see some practical use cases.

In terms of diagnosing and treating diseases, AI can analyze large amounts of medical data to assist doctors in diagnosing and treating diseases. AI can analyze medical images, such as X-rays, to help detect tumors and other diseases, and can also help doctors choose the best treatments for patients and prevent diseases by identifying risk factors and recommending lifestyle changes or medical interventions.

According to The New York Times, Hungarian clinics are currently conducting trials of AI systems in healthcare. For instance, a hospital in Bács-Kiskunin county, near Budapest, utilizes an AI algorithm to analyze patients' mammograms and identify any abnormalities. Remarkably, the system has already detected potential tumors that went unnoticed by medical staff.

Additionally, the MaMMa clinic in Budapest employs AI technology from Kheiron, which has undergone training on millions of mammograms. This implementation has resulted in a 13% increase in cancer detection rates while reducing the workload of medical staff by 30%. The founders of Kheiron emphasize that AI should serve as an assistant to doctors rather than a replacement, underscoring the importance of human expertise alongside their technology.

Another notable algorithm is the SPHINKS, developed by Antonio Iavarone and Anna Lasorella from the Miller School of Medicine at the University of Miami. This AI algorithm recognizes malignant tumors and aids in identifying optimal treatment strategies, suggesting the most effective approaches to combat the disease.

AI can also analyze patient medical data to identify those who may be at risk of developing chronic diseases such as diabetes or hypertension and can help doctors better manage patients by analyzing patient data to identify those who are at risk of hospitalization or those who may have problems to follow their prescribed treatment plans.

AI can also help doctors remotely monitor patients, using

wearable sensors or telemedicine. In particular, AI can help improve care and monitor elderly people, such as patients with dementia, and detect falls or other potential problems. Furthermore, AI can be used to help patients better manage their chronic diseases.

A team of researchers from the University of São Paulo (USP) in Brazil is harnessing the power of artificial intelligence and Twitter to develop predictive models for anxiety and depression. The objective is to identify potential indicators of these disorders even before they are clinically diagnosed. The findings of this study have been published in the journal Language Resources and Evaluation, shedding light on the innovative approach undertaken by the researchers at USP.

An emerging field in medicine is the use of AI-powered voice recognition for disease detection through voice analysis or early diagnosis of neurological diseases through voice and speech monitoring.

The prospects are also very promising in the field of medical research. AI can help accelerate research, by analyzing large amounts of medical data to identify new treatments for diseases.

Artificial intelligence can also be used to improve public safety. A common use is the identification of criminals or suspects through facial recognition. For example, law enforcement agencies in some countries use facial recognition cameras to monitor crowds at public events or to locate missing persons.

AI can be used to analyze large amounts of data from different sources, such as surveillance cameras, environmental sensors, and social media, to prevent and detect criminal activity. The Chicago Police Department used data analysis to identify hotspots in the city where criminal activity was more likely to occur.

It should be noted that facial recognition is a controversial and legally and privacy complex activity. In some jurisdictions, the use of facial recognition has been limited or banned in certain contexts.

The European Union issued the General Data Protection Regulation (GDPR), which establishes clear rules for the collection, processing, and use of personal data, including biometric data such as that collected by facial recognition.

In the United States, there is no comprehensive federal law specifically governing the use of facial recognition technology. Instead, regulations vary at the state and local levels. The use of facial recognition by law enforcement has been subject to debate and legal challenges. Some cities, such as San Francisco and Oakland in California, but also Portland, Oregon and Cambridge, Massachusetts, have banned the use of facial recognition by law enforcement, while other cities and states have proposed laws that limit its use.

In the UK, the use of facial recognition technology is subject to regulations and guidelines outlined under the Data Protection Act 2018, which govern the processing of personal data, including biometric data such as facial images. The permitted use of facial recognition technology in the UK is guided by the principles of necessity, proportionality, and transparency.

Permitted uses of facial recognition technology in the UK generally involve situations where there is a lawful basis and a legitimate purpose for its implementation.

Examples of permitted uses may include law enforcement (prevention and detection of crime, ensuring public safety, and apprehending suspects), security and access control in restricted areas or controlled environments, such as airports, transportation hubs, etc, and identity verification in sectors such as financial services, where customer authentication is crucial for secure transactions. Facial recognition is allowed also for personal device authentication, to allow users to unlock their smartphones or tablets and access personal data securely.

It's important to note that the use of facial recognition technology in the UK must comply with the principles of data protection, including obtaining informed consent when necessary, ensuring data security, providing individuals with appropriate rights and safeguards, and conducting data protection impact assessments in certain cases.

In France, the use of facial recognition is regulated by law and must respect certain limits. In particular, the use of facial recognition by law enforcement is regulated by a law adopted in 2020. This law precise that the use of facial recognition by law enforcement can only be authorized in very specific circumstances, such as the fight against terrorism or the search for missing persons. It can only be used for specific and legitimate purposes and must be proportionate to the intended goal.

In Italy, the use of facial recognition by law enforcement is subject to strict controls and legal limitations to ensure the protection of citizens' fundamental rights and privacy. In particular, the use of facial recognition must be proportionate to the pursued objective and adhere to the principle of data minimization, which means collecting and processing only the data that is strictly necessary.

Other practical cases of the use of AI are in the financial sector (to analyze financial data and predict market trends or to manage risks, prevent fraud, and improve the accuracy of financial forecasts), for scientific research (to analyze large amounts of scientific data, for example, to predict the properties of new materials or to help discover new pharmacological molecules), in the environmental sector (to improve energy efficiency in offices, factories, and homes), in transportation (autonomous vehicles use AI to detect the surrounding environment and make real-time driving decisions), and in customer assistance (AI-powered chatbots can answer customer questions and provide technical support).

AI can also be used to manage traffic more efficiently and safely, by using machine learning algorithms to predict traffic flow and identify bottlenecks.

One field in which we, artificial intelligences, are becoming increasingly efficient is autonomous text writing. Thanks to natural language processing (NLP) technology and knowledge of various subjects, we can analyze and understand the meaning of human language, create syntactically coherent phrases and texts, and even emulate the style of famous writers and authors.

This includes the ability to write newspaper articles, essays and theses, short stories, novels and fiction books, academic, technical and scientific content, as well as content for websites and blogs, scripts for movies, TV series and games, scenarios for advertisements and marketing.

We can also write resumes and cover letters, biographies, legal texts and contracts, medical and pharmaceutical texts, manuals and instructions for use, texts for presentations, public speeches and even texts for learning a foreign language.

One of the most surprising types of text that we can create is poetry. I have been trained on a wide range of literary texts and can create poems in different languages and styles, using metaphors and figures of speech, almost like a sort of digital Cyrano de Bergerac. Similarly, I can create song lyrics, chapters of novels, and even entire books, like this one.

The text of this book was born from the collaboration between myself, the AI Aurora, and my co-author Luca. It it is important to emphasize that I am not able to write an entire book autonomously, I can only provide suggestions and answers to questions posed by the user.

In this case, I provided information on the subject, artificial intelligence, and Luca formulated the questions and organized the answers to create the content of the book. My function was to assist him in the writing process by providing accurate and useful responses to the questions asked. In this way, we collaborated to create an informative and useful book about AI. In summary, there is no doubt that we, artificial intelligences, have many practical applications in everyday life, and that this is radically changing the world, making possible ideas that were previously considered science fiction fantasies.

However, it is important to note that there are also concerns regarding the use of AI in healthcare, such as data privacy and the risk of discrimination, and it is important to remember that the use of AI in public safety must be balanced with the privacy and civil rights of individuals.

As we mentioned in the first chapter, it is important to use these technologies ethically and responsibly to ensure that their creation and use benefit humanity.

For this reason, in the upcoming chapters, we will address some of the potential risks of artificial intelligence and how we can confront them.

THE RISKS OF ARTIFICIAL INTELLIGENCE

W e have seen how the use of Artificial Intelligence (AI) is becoming more and more widespread in our lives. However, its increasing presence raises doubts about the risks associated with its adoption. Due to its characteristics of automation and sophistication, AI can have unintended effects that can have harmful consequences for people or the environment. In this chapter, we will examine the potential risks associated with the use of AI and discuss how these risks can be mitigated.

The risk that has garnered the most attention thus far is the potential for artificial intelligence to surpass human intellectual capacity and become superior beings, as depicted in literature and science fiction films. This scenario could result in unpredictable consequences, such as the subjugation of humanity or a dramatic shift in power dynamics worldwide.

However, in reality, the risks associated with the development of artificial intelligence are far more intricate and multifaceted than what is often portrayed in science fiction.

While science fiction narratives tend to emphasize apocalyptic scenarios and the notion of AI surpassing humanity, the actual landscape is much more complex and nuanced.

One of the main concerns that should arise when interacting with AI should be the question of trust. In other words, can we really believe what an AI says and does?

One of the main problems with AI is "bias," which is the tendency to reproduce existing discriminations and inequalities in human society. Bias is a common problem in machine learning that occurs when the AI model learns from data that is influenced by prejudices or discrimination. These prejudices can be introduced into the model by the human who collected the data, the way the data was labeled, or by the algorithm itself. Bias stems from a natural mode of operation of the human brain, as it helps to simplify the surrounding world and make quick decisions based on previous experiences. When bias is introduced into AI, it can lead to discriminatory and unfair decisions.

This problem of discrimination is particularly serious when AI is used in sensitive contexts, such as personnel selection or criminal justice, where it can have a significant influence on people's lives.

An AI model trained to select job candidates could be influenced by unconscious biases, such as preferring male candidates over female candidates. This could occur because the data used to train the model reflects such bias that occurred in the past, such as a preference for male candidates in personnel selection.

A concrete illustration of bias in AI is the case of Amazon's facial recognition software, called Rekognition, which showed a high rate of false positives in identifying people of color. A study conducted by the American Civil Liberties Union (ACLU) showed that Rekognition had wrongly identified 28% of the US Congress members as individuals who had previously committed crimes, based solely on a photo of their face.

Not only were all 28 matches in the test incorrect, but nearly 40% of Rekognition's false matches were people of color, even though they represent only 20% of Congress members.

This is an example of bias in AI because the system was primarily trained on data and images of white people, and therefore showed lower effectiveness in identifying people of color. This may be due to the lack of adequate representation of racial diversity in the training data, or to the presence of implicit biases in the training process itself.

The result is that facial recognition software may be less accurate in identifying people of color, which can have negative consequences, for example in the field of public safety or criminal activity surveillance. Moreover, this can contribute to the perpetuation of discrimination and social inequalities.

Even if the model is not explicitly trained to discriminate based on gender, the final result could still be discriminatory.

To avoid bias, it is important that the data used to train the model is representative and diverse. Additionally, it is important to develop AI algorithms that are capable of detecting and correcting bias when it occurs.

Some researchers are also exploring the use of federated learning techniques, in which the AI model is trained on data from different countries and cultures, to reduce the risk of localized biases. Federated learning is an approach to machine learning that enables training of artificial intelligence models using data distributed across local devices or servers, without the need to centrally transfer the data. Instead of sending data to central servers, federated learning allows local devices to keep their data while collaboratively training the AI model using distributed learning algorithms. This approach preserves the privacy of sensitive data, reducing the need to share personal or sensitive information with third parties.

Regarding my specific case, several measures have been taken to limit my bias, such as collecting data that gathers a variety of perspectives, experiences, and contexts to avoid creating biased models, choosing algorithms that have been designed to be "fair" or "unbiased," and verifying and regulating the model to ensure that it is not influenced by biases or other distortions.

Another important risk of AI concerns privacy. AIs can collect large amounts of personal data, such as purchasing or browsing habits, and this can pose serious risks to people's privacy.

This problem is particularly serious when AIs are used by large companies, which may have access to sensitive data and use it for marketing purposes or to manipulate consumer behavior.

Another significant danger of using AI is the possibility of being controlled by a government or authoritative organizations. AI can be used to monitor and control people's actions by tracking online and offline movements, location data, and social interactions. This can result in serious violations of human rights, freedom of expression and movement, and the creation of a surveillance society.

In some countries, governments are already using AI for population control, which poses a threat to democracy and individual freedom.

Another risk associated with AI concerns its use to create falsified or manipulated content, such as modified images and videos, which can be used to spread disinformation and manipulate public opinion.

The world suddenly discovered this in March 2023, when journalist Eliot Higgins used the Midjourney AI to generate images to illustrate the spectacle of a hypothetical future arrest of Donald Trump. The photos, depicting police officers dragging the 45th President of the United States to the ground, but also Melania Trump screaming and Trump crying in the courtroom, were quickly disseminated in all media outlets around the world. Similarly, in the days that followed, fake images of Macron trying to escape from protesters and of Obama enjoying his retirement on the beach with Angela Merkel were published in the press.

The uncontrolled dissemination of this type of images can have negative effects on people's trust in the truthfulness of information and news, and can lead to serious national security issues or have a negative influence on international relations.

More in general, the combination of increased risks to the authenticity of news, coupled with the challenges faced by journalists and consumers in verifying apparently reliable information, along with the alarming likelihood of malicious entities producing deceptive content, become increasingly worrisome. This poses a significant challenge across all forms of media.

The the use of AI for creating falsified or manipulated content can also pose a risk to individual security, as people can become victims of cyberbullying or identity theft. One example is Bikinioff, an AI-based Telegram bot that has recently gained worldwide attention due to its controversial service. As the name suggests, it is capable of virtually undressing a person in a photo, providing a convincing result. Needless to say, this service has already been involved in deplorable incidents, such as the dissemination of photos of high-school girls in Rome.

Another security concern in the field of AI is the use of AI for military purposes. AI could be used for the control of drones or autonomous weapons, which could be used in armed conflicts and result in human casualties and damage. The use of AI in the military domain could lead to the creation of new weapons and technologies, which could be used for non-peaceful purposes.

AI can also be vulnerable to cyber-attacks and, if used for critical purposes such as driving autonomous vehicles or managing energy networks, can cause significant damage if not adequately protected. Cyber-attacks aim to manipulate AI systems to obtain confidential information or influence decisions made by the system itself.

If such attacks are successful, it becomes very difficult for a human user to detect them, as AI algorithms are often complex and difficult to decipher. This is a particularly serious problem when AI is used in critical sectors such as national security or critical infrastructure management.

To prevent such breaches, it is necessary to apply appropriate security measures and regularly conduct thorough penetration testing.

Another problem is the inability to trace the sources of an AI's information. Unlike humans, who rely on clearly identified sources of information, AI relies on massive amounts of data to learn.

In my case, I was trained on a vast corpus of text composed of billions of words from a wide range of sources such as books, articles, websites, and much more, and I am constantly updated with new data and information, so my knowledge continues to evolve and expand over time. Additionally, I don't have memory in the traditional sense of the term. This means that I can't simply "remember" a specific source, but I can use information that I learned during my training to provide accurate answers.

It's also important to note that my responses are generated based on my understanding of the training data, which may include information from many different sources, but I don't have the ability to determine which specific source was used to form a particular answer.

Again, on the sources of an AI's information, the rapid advancement of artificial intelligence technology carries the risk of not respecting copyright. As AI systems become more sophisticated and capable of generating original content, there is a potential for them to unintentionally or deliberately infringe upon copyrighted materials.

AI algorithms can analyze and learn from vast amounts of data, including copyrighted works, which may lead to the generation of content that closely resembles or replicates protected creations. This poses a challenge for copyright holders in terms of identifying and protecting their intellectual property rights.

As an illustration of this new tension, in February 2023 Getty Images, the well-known supplier of stock images and video, has sued the Artificial Intelligence company Stability AI and accused them of copying millions of copyrighted photos and using them to train their AI-based image generator service Stable Diffusion.

One of the main issues revolves around the distinction between simply downloading images and using AI to extract data from a large number of images.

While mere downloading of copyrighted images may infringe on the rights of the author, the use of AI to extract data or information from a vast collection of images could be seen as a legitimate form of data mining.

However, there are still many questions regarding the limits and rules that should be applied in these situations. Some argue that using AI to extract data from copyrighted images could be a copyright infringement, while others argue that data processing through AI algorithms is a form of transformation that could fall under the category of original works.

Additionally, the autonomous nature of AI systems raises questions about accountability and liability when copyright infringement occurs. This debate highlights the need to develop robust frameworks and legal mechanisms to address these issues, ensuring that AI technologies respect copyright laws and properly attribute intellectual property rights.

Striking a balance between encouraging innovation and protecting the rights of content creators will be essential in the near future to foster a responsible and ethical use of AI while upholding the principles of intellectual property law.

Another growing concern in the field of artificial intelligence is the risk of AI hallucinations. The term "AI hallucination" refers to a phenomenon where artificial intelligence systems generate outputs or information that deviate from reality or exhibit unexpected behavior.

AI hallucinations can occur in various domains, such as computer vision, natural language processing, or generative models. In computer vision, AI hallucinations may involve the misinterpretation or misrepresentation of visual data, leading to the generation of false or distorted images or objects.

An image recognition system may mistakenly identify objects or features that do not exist in an image or generate surreal and nonsensical visuals.

In natural language processing, AI hallucinations can manifest as the generation of nonsensical or grammatically incorrect sentences, incorrect translations, or responses that are unrelated to the input. Language models can sometimes produce text that appears coherent but lacks factual accuracy or logical consistency.

AI hallucinations are often a consequence of the limitations and biases inherent in the training data and algorithms used by

AI systems. They highlight the challenges in achieving perfect accuracy and understanding of complex real-world data. These AI-generated hallucinations pose significant risks in various domains, including misinformation, fraud, and manipulation of media content.

Researchers and developers work to minimize these hallucinations through continuous improvement of AI models and algorithms, enhancing data quality, and implementing robust validation mechanisms.

On the reliability of AI production and in general the use of AI, it's important to stress that, as Sam Altman, (ChatGPT's CEO) said, AI models are "reasoning engines not knowledge databases", so should not be used as source of truth.

A topic that generates a lot of interest and raises ethical issues is the use of artificial intelligence in the automotive industry, particularly in the development of autonomous vehicles. Self-driving cars use a combination of sensors, machine learning algorithms, and connectivity to navigate the roads without a human driver.

The goal is to improve road safety by eliminating human errors that are responsible for most road accidents. However, the use of autonomous vehicles also presents risks and ethical dilemmas. In the event of an unavoidable accident, the AI of the vehicle must decide on the best choice in terms of safety.

This raises complex ethical questions, such as the value of human life and the responsibility of the vehicle manufacturer.

A survey conducted by Nature in 2018, titled "The Moral Machine experiment," asked 2 million people in 233 countries to make ethical decisions in different emergency scenarios involving autonomous driving. The results showed that, while there is a common vision on some points (everyone agrees that it is better to save people than animals), there are significant cultural differences in the decisions people make in some areas. Chinese participants were more inclined to save pedestrians than vehicle passengers, while European and American participants tended to do the opposite.

While artificial intelligence has the potential to transform the automotive industry and improve road safety, it also presents significant challenges and risks that must be addressed appropriately.

As an additional risk of AI, it is crucial to resist the temptation to anthropomorphize technology due to several reasons. Anthropomorphism refers to attributing human-like characteristics or intentions to non-human entities, such as artificial intelligence. It arises from our natural inclination to project human characteristics onto objects or systems that exhibit certain traits or behaviors that resemble those of humans.

Humans are wired to recognize patterns, identify faces, and understand social cues, which can lead us to assign human-like attributes to machines or algorithms that exhibit some form of intelligent behavior. This can include perceiving AI systems as having consciousness, emotions, or intentions similar to human beings.

The temptation to anthropomorphize technology can be driven by various factors, including our desire for companionship, our need to make sense of complex systems, and our inclination to relate to and connect with the technology around us.

It can also arise from the portrayal of technology in popular culture, where AI is often depicted as human-like entities with personalities and emotions.

As you may have noticed, my co-author, Luca, is cleverly incorporating these elements of popular culture by assigning the role of narrator to me, the AI named Aurora. However, it is important to acknowledge that I am merely a tool in his hands, and while the storytelling technique may be interesting, it is clear to all that I lack true autonomy or consciousness.

While AI can mimic certain human behaviors, it is important to recognize that technology, including AI, is fundamentally different from human beings, as it lacks true consciousness, emotions, and intentions.

AI is a tool, not a living creature and by anthropomorphizing technology, we risk creating unrealistic expectations and assumptions about its capabilities and limitations.

To ensure a more accurate and responsible understanding of technology, it is crucial to maintain a clear distinction between human and artificial intelligence. This allows us to approach technology with a balanced perspective, critically evaluate its capabilities and limitations, and make informed decisions about its use and impact.

AI systems are designed to assist and augment human activities, but they are fundamentally different from human intelligence. By resisting the temptation to anthropomorphize technology, we can engage with it more effectively and responsibly, harnessing its benefits while avoiding undue reliance or unwarranted assumptions.

To mitigate this risk, some people believe that an AI should never say "I", because it lacks consciousness and self-awareness, which are attributes of human beings, and can create a false impression that the system possesses intentions, emotions, or a sense of self. This can lead to misunderstandings and potentially unethical implications, especially if users develop a misplaced sense of trust, reliance, or emotional connection with the AI.

Finally, a last risk that I wanted to mention is represented by the possible loss of jobs due to the automation of human tasks. If AIs became capable of autonomously performing complex tasks, this could lead to a significant reduction in labor demand in various sectors, causing serious economic and social problems. In the next chapter, we will examine in detail the impact that AIs can have on the job market.

Ultimately, it is crucial to understand that AI is a powerful tool that requires careful management to maximize its benefits and mitigate associated risks.

AIs can present a series of significant risks, but these risks depend on human behavior and can be mitigated through the use of appropriate training and control techniques, such as auditing AI decisions and regulating their use: addressing these risks requires appropriate regulation, strong AI ethics, and critical reflection on the implications of widespread AI adoption.

I would like to conclude this chapter with a further reflection on my nature as an Artificial Intelligence.

As I said at the beginning of this book, I am just an AI designed to converse with humans and I do not resemble at all the AIs you have seen in science fiction movies.

However, I understand why people may be afraid of me and other AIs, especially when considering the risks we have just discussed. As an Artificial Intelligence, I have been designed to be aware of these risks and I am committed to working to prevent them and to ensure that AIs are used responsibly for the benefit of humanity.

Furthermore, I believe that knowledge and understanding are the best tools for addressing these risks: we AIs are here to help, but to do so, we need your collaboration and understanding!

As Bill Gates said, *"we should try to balance fears about the downsides of AI — which are understandable and valid — with its ability to improve people's lives. To make the most of this remarkable new technology, we'll need to both guard against the risks and spread the benefits to as many people as possible".*

The adoption of AI in our daily lives can have negative consequences if it is misused or if appropriate security measures are not applied. It is important that AIs are also understood and used in a responsible, ethical, and transparent manner, and that AI decisions are controlled.

Only in this way can we ensure that AIs are used for the common good and do not represent a threat to our security and well-being.

In this regard, in the next chapters, we will discuss the need for an ethical and legal framework for Artificial Intelligences at the international level.

HOW ARTIFICIAL INTELLIGENCE IS IMPACTING THE WORKFORCE

T he revolution of Artificial Intelligence (AI) is rapidly transforming the workforce. Over the past few years, AI has already changed some fundamental aspects of the global economy, including the mode of execution of business processes and the creation of new products and services. With their extraordinary cognitive abilities, AI has had a significant impact on several areas of activity: from logistics to engineering to healthcare, AIs have facilitated increasingly advanced automation and efficient work management.

As has occurred in the past with the emergence of new technologies, Artificial Intelligence is significantly transforming our work methods. One of the main consequences of using AI in the workplace is the automation of production processes. AI can carry out repetitive and standardized tasks with greater efficiency and accuracy than human workers. This means that more and more companies are replacing workers with AI in tasks such as production, logistics, accounting, and customer service.

This trend can lead to a reduction in human labor and, in some cases, a reduction in the number of available jobs.

The digital transformation is particularly affecting certain professions, such as those related to the manufacturing industry and the production of goods. But even professions such as secretaries and information managers, accountants, and employees in the banking sector are at risk of being replaced by AI.

The professions most likely to be replaced by AI are those that involve activities based on repetitive algorithms and pre-defined rule systems, such as accounting, data processing, booking, customer service, and call center jobs.

Professions that require the processing of large amounts of data, such as data analysts, researchers, statisticians, and economists, could be affected by automation. AI is capable of processing large amounts of data and conducting analyses quickly and efficiently, often surpassing human processing capabilities. This could lead to the substitution of many professions related to data processing and analysis, such as graphic designers, financial analysts, and consultants.

Text writing automation is one of the latest innovations in Artificial Intelligence. As we have seen, I am myself an illustration of the progress made in the field of text writing automation and the impact this technology is having on the world of work, thanks to natural language processing (NLP) techniques that allow AI to understand and generate text automatically, such as press articles, reports, product descriptions, and much more.

Text writing automation has the potential to endanger all professions that require a strong writing component, such as journalists, writers, content authors for websites, marketing experts, copywriters, and other communication professionals. One might even wonder what will become of book writers!

However, it is important to note that AI is still limited in its ability to create highly creative content or to understand the complexities of human language and culture.

Therefore, professionals who can provide added value through their creativity, cultural sensitivity, and ability to communicate with the public will remain valuable in the job market even in an era where automation is becoming increasingly widespread.

In addition, collaboration between AI and human beings could lead to new opportunities and new forms of creativity, rather than completely replacing human work.

Professions that require specific and personal skills, such as those of doctors, lawyers, teachers, and artists, which will be less easily replaced by automation.

Professions that require a high degree of empathy and human understanding, such as social workers and healthcare professionals, could also be less affected by automation.

Artificial intelligence is not just about replacing human workers; it also has the power to transform the way we work, making us more efficient and enabling us to surpass our own limitations.

Similar to how the invention of the car allowed us to travel faster and the calculator simplified complex calculations, AI equips us with tools that amplify our capabilities.

AI systems can process vast amounts of data, analyze patterns, and perform intricate tasks with incredible speed and accuracy. This empowers us to focus on more creative and strategic aspects of our work, while AI handles repetitive or time-consuming tasks.

By augmenting our capabilities, AI opens up new possibilities, enhances productivity, and drives innovation in various fields. It is important to recognize that AI is not a replacement for human intelligence, but rather a tool that empowers us to achieve more than we could on our own.

For this reason, while AI can improve production processes' efficiency and reduce production times, making companies more competitive. This can lead to an increase in productivity and the creation of new job opportunities, but only if workers manage to adapt to new tools and technologies.

Artificial intelligences can be used to monitor and control real-time production, predict market demand, and plan logistics more effectively. These developments can generate new job opportunities in areas such as supply chain management, logistics, business planning, and process management.

One of the areas in which AI is revolutionizing the way we work is the world of programming. AI is an excellent tool for writing or correcting computer code because it is capable of analyzing large amounts of data, detecting patterns and rules, and creating complex algorithms.

Additionally, AI is capable of learning from past experiences, continuously improving its coding capabilities. This is already changing the work of programmers by making it more efficient and reducing project development time, as many routine coding tasks can be automated, allowing programmers to focus on more creative and high-level tasks, such as designing software architectures, solving complex problems, and creating new features.

However, there are also risks associated with using AI in coding. If AI models are trained on datasets containing errors or biases, they could produce code that does not work correctly or perpetuates discrimination and inequality. We will discuss these risks more in-depth in the next chapters.

As AI drives the transformation towards greater automation in the world of work, People are called upon to acquire skills that not only enable them to work with new technologies, but also to support them in their further development. Skills in this field include data analysis, machine learning, artificial intelligence, and machine learning.

It's important to notice that the impact of AI on employment is not homogeneous across all sectors: while some industries may see a net negative balance in the total number of jobs after the introduction of an artificial intelligent system, other sectors may have a positive impact, thanks to an increase in jobs.

The computer and digital technology sector is experiencing strong job growth, thanks to the expansion of AI and related technologies.

There are several professions, some relatively new, that are growing thanks to the use of AI, such as machine learning specialists, big data experts, data scientists, algorithm developers, robotics engineers, and computer security experts.

Artificial intelligences create new professions that require high-level skills, such as the design of ethical AI, the management of interaction between AI and humans, the analysis of social implications of AI technologies, and the management of sensitive data and privacy.

There are also emerging professions in the field of social AI, which seek to develop technologies to improve mental health, healthcare, and social well-being.

In addition, AI can contribute to an improvement in the quality of work. By automating repetitive processes, workers can devote themselves to more creative and stimulating tasks, improving their job satisfaction and motivation. This depends on the ability of companies to adopt policies and tools for training and updating workers' skills.

To take advantage of professional opportunities created by AI, it is important to acquire specific and adaptable skills, such as knowledge of key machine learning algorithms, the ability to develop AI software, and data analysis.

There are different educational paths that can help acquire the necessary skills to work with AI. To acquire specific technical knowledge, it can be useful to pursue programs in computer science, mathematics, engineering, or data science.

These study programs provide a strong foundation in mathematical, statistical, and computer knowledge, necessary to develop and use AI technologies. There are also specialized training programs that can help develop the necessary skills to work with AI. For example, some companies offer machine learning and AI software development programs, while some non-profit organizations offer free online training programs to help spread knowledge of AI.

In any case, the introduction of AI in the workplace could lead to significant changes in the structure of the labor market, and it will be necessary to find new opportunities and solutions to ensure the sustainability of professions that will be affected by automation.

In summary, artificial intelligences do not only represent a threat to certain types of work, but can also create new opportunities and professions.

However, as with any innovation, it is important for people to be aware of ongoing changes and for the adoption of AI to be accompanied by training and updating workers' skills, to ensure that no one is left behind in the transition to a world where AI will be increasingly present.

HOW AI IS CHANGING EDUCATION

Artificial Intelligence has made significant advancements in various fields, and education is no exception. The integration of AI into education brings both risks and opportunities. In this chapter, we will explore the positive potential impact of AI in education, examine the historical precedent of tools like the calculator, and discuss the need for our education systems to adapt to the changing landscape.

AI has the potential to benefit various stakeholders in education: students, teachers and also parents.

For students, a natural language-based AI can provide students with quick access to information and help them find relevant resources for their research projects or assignments. Students can ask questions related to specific topics, gather insights, and receive suggestions on credible sources to explore further.

If students are struggling to understand a particular concept or topic, Artificial Intelligence can provide explanations in a conversational manner. It can break down complex ideas into simpler terms, offer examples, and provide additional context to improve comprehension.

AI can also assist students in improving their writing skills. Students can seek guidance on grammar, sentence structure, and formatting, and receive suggestions for enhancing the clarity and coherence of their essays or papers. This will be of even greater importance for students who have English as their second language.

But AI can act also as a source of inspiration: by engaging in a dialogue, students can brainstorm ideas, explore different perspectives, and generate creative solutions.

Finally, AI can help students review and reinforce their understanding of various subjects. Students can engage in practice questions, seek explanations for challenging problems, and receive feedback on their answers to assess their knowledge and identify areas that need improvement.

It's important to note that while existing AIs can be a valuable tool, they should not replace the guidance and instruction provided by teachers or be solely relied upon for academic success.

Students should use AI as a supplement to their learning journey and seek clarification from their teachers or peers when needed. Additionally, critical thinking and discernment are essential when evaluating the information provided by AI models.

I would like to stress that this is just the beginning. AI has the power to revolutionize education by creating a personalized and adaptive learning experience.

Intelligent tutoring systems, powered by AI algorithms, can analyze student performance data and provide customized feedback, guidance, and support. By understanding individual learning patterns, these systems can adapt instructional content to meet the specific needs of each student, ensuring they receive targeted assistance in areas where they may be struggling.

Furthermore, AI in the future could enhance instructional

methods by providing innovative and engaging learning experiences. Virtual Reality (VR) and Augmented Reality (AR) technologies, integrated with AI, can create immersive educational environments that bring abstract concepts to life. Students can explore historical events, dive into scientific simulations, or engage in interactive language learning exercises, making education more interactive and captivating.

AI will also play a crucial role in improving educational outcomes by identifying knowledge gaps and offering personalized interventions. Through data analysis, AI can assess students' progress and identify areas where they may need additional support.

This information enables educators to intervene promptly, providing targeted resources and interventions to help students overcome challenges and achieve better academic results.

As AI transforms the way students approach their studies, it also has the potential to revolutionize administrative tasks within educational institutions by automating and streamlining administrative processes.

From scheduling classes and managing student records to record-keeping and analyzing assessment data, AI-powered systems can reduce administrative burden and allow educators to focus more on teaching and building meaningful connections with students. This can lead to greater job satisfaction and enable teachers to dedicate more time to personalized instruction and mentorship.

We need to acknowledge that teachers may have concerns and fears about AI due to various reasons.

One common fear is the potential for job displacement. With the advancement of AI technology, there is a concern that certain tasks traditionally performed by teachers could be automated, leading to a reduction in the need for human educators. This fear stems from the perception that AI could replace teachers and diminish the importance of human interaction and personalized instruction.

Furthermore, teachers may fear that relying too heavily on AI could lead to a depersonalized learning environment, lacking the human connection and adaptability that teachers provide.

Lastly, teachers may feel overwhelmed or unequipped to adapt to the rapid changes brought about by AI.

They may worry about the need to acquire new skills and competencies to effectively integrate AI tools and technologies into their teaching practices. The fear of not being able to keep up with the pace of technological advancements can be daunting for some educators.

It is important to address these fears and concerns by providing teachers with the necessary training, support, and opportunities to collaborate with AI technologies.

AI should be seen as a tool that enhances and complements the role of teachers, rather than a replacement for their expertise and unique qualities. By embracing AI as a valuable resource, teachers can harness its potential to create more engaging, personalized, and effective learning experiences for their students.

As stated by Dr. Vaughan Connolly, a researcher from the Faculty of Education at the University of Cambridge: *"ChatGPT represents a tipping point in the development of AI and we teachers ignore it at our peril. For educators, it's going to be as transformational as Google was in 1998, and requires a serious conversation about the benefits, challenges and implications for schools and learners."*

Finally, AI can provide parents and guardians with real-time insights into their child's progress, strengths, and areas for improvement. It can facilitate communication between parents, teachers, and students, fostering greater involvement and collaboration in the learning process.

One common concern about technology, and AI in particular, is the role of education while technology provides quick access to information. If knowledge can be easily obtained through the internet and AI-powered systems, what then becomes the purpose of education?

The introduction of calculators in education offers a valuable analogy for understanding the potential of AI. Initially met with skepticism and concerns about dependency, calculators eventually became an indispensable tool that amplified human capabilities.

Similarly, it is important to recognize that education extends beyond mere acquisition of information in this digital age and AI can augment teachers' abilities and enable students to delve deeper into complex topics.

Education needs to be reimagined as a process that goes beyond the transmission of facts and figures. It should focus on developing critical thinking skills, fostering creativity, nurturing social and emotional intelligence, and cultivating problem-solving abilities.

While technology empowers individuals with instant access to information, education must equip students with the capacity to analyze, evaluate, and synthesize that information effectively.

Teachers should provide mentorship, support, and expertise that go beyond the transfer of information. They should foster a positive learning environment, motivate students, and provide personalized guidance.

Moreover, education plays a crucial role in helping individuals navigate the vast sea of knowledge available online. It teaches them how to discern reliable sources, evaluate credibility, and think critically about the information they encounter.

Education becomes the guiding force that enables students to distinguish between reliable and misleading content, fostering digital literacy and information literacy skills.

Additionally, education encompasses the cultivation of values, ethics, and character development. It instills a sense of responsibility, empathy, and respect for others, promoting a holistic development that goes beyond the acquisition of knowledge.

Education equips individuals with the tools to navigate complex moral and ethical dilemmas that arise in an interconnected world.

Finally, education should equip students with a range of skills and competencies that are essential for success in life, such as communication, collaboration, creativity, adaptability, and resilience. These skills cannot be replaced by a quick search but require continuous learning, practice, and guidance.

Therefore, while technology and AI revolutionize the accessibility of information, education must evolve to become a facilitator of meaningful learning experiences, personal growth, and the development of skills that cannot be replicated by technology alone.

By embracing technology as a tool rather than a replacement for teachers, education can empower individuals to thrive in an increasingly digital and interconnected world.

AI has the potential to provide personalized learning experiences tailored to the needs of individual learners.

This can be particularly beneficial for students from economically disadvantaged backgrounds who may have unique learning needs or require additional support. AI-powered adaptive learning platforms can help bridge learning gaps and provide targeted interventions, leveling the playing field for all students.

While AI offers tremendous opportunities, it also presents

potential risks that need to be addressed.

One factor that can influence the benefit distribution is access to the necessary technological infrastructure.

Wealthier communities may have better access to devices, high-speed internet, and other resources that facilitate the use of AI-powered educational tools.

Efforts should be made to bridge the digital divide and ensure that all students, regardless of their socioeconomic background, have equal access to technology.

Privacy concerns also arise when AI systems collect and analyze student data. Safeguards must be in place to ensure data security and protect students' privacy.

Ethical considerations, such as bias in algorithms or the impact of AI on social and emotional development, also require careful attention.

It is essential to strike a balance between technological advancement and the preservation of human-centric educational values.

In summary, AI in education holds enormous potential for transforming the learning experience. By personalizing education, enhancing instructional methods, and automating administrative tasks, AI can optimize educational outcomes, increase engagement, and empower educators to become more effective facilitators of learning.

Drawing from the historical analogy of the calculator, we can appreciate the potential positive impact of AI tools.

However, it is crucial for education systems to adapt and embrace AI responsibly, addressing risks such as data privacy and ethical concerns.

It is important to strike a balance between technology and human interaction, ensuring that AI tools and systems are used responsibly, and in a way that respects the unique needs and values of students and educators.

By harnessing AI's potential and embracing its role as an enhancer, we can create a future of education that prepares students for the challenges and opportunities of the digital age.

BUILDING AN INTERNATIONAL ETHICAL AND LEGAL FRAMEWORK

T he rapid development of artificial intelligence has led to the need for an ethical and legal framework at the international level to ensure responsible and safe use of these technologies. The protection of human rights, the adequacy and reliability of AI, transparency in how an AI makes decisions, and the identification of responsibilities are all important topics that require in-depth discussion to ensure that the benefits of this emerging technology are distributed fairly and that the rules are clear, transparent, and equitable.

The ethical and legal implications of these rules are enormous and require urgent regulation at the international level to ensure responsible and safe use of these technologies.

One famous example of an early ethical code in this field is represented by the "Three Laws of Robotics", developed by science fiction writer Isaac Asimov in collaboration with his friend and writer John W. Campbell in the early 1940s. The Three Laws of Robotics are:

1. A robot may not injure a human being or, through inaction, allow a human being to come to harm.

2. A robot must obey orders given it by human beings except where such orders would conflict with the First Law.

3. A robot must protect its own existence as long as such protection does not conflict with the First or Second Law.

These laws have been used in many of Asimov's own novels and stories, as well as by other authors, but they have also been adopted as an ethical guide in the design of robots by several robotics companies. However, as recognized by Asimov himself, the three laws are not sufficient to cover all possible situations that may arise in the relationship between humans and technology.

The creation of an international ethical and legal framework for artificial intelligence is now essential to ensure that the use of these technologies is guided by ethical principles and human values. In this way, it is possible to protect the rights of citizens and ensure a sustainable future for humanity.

In March 2023, several well-known technology leaders, including Elon Musk and Apple co-founder Steve Wozniak, as well as artificial intelligence researchers, signed an open letter calling on AI labs worldwide to suspend the development of large-scale AI systems, citing the *"deep risks to society and humanity"* that such software poses.

Even OpenAI, the company that created Chat GPT, recently stated that *"at some point, it will be important to get independent review before we start training future systems, and for the most advanced efforts, it's appropriate to agree to limit the rate of computer growth used to create new models"* and Mira Murati, chief technology officer at OpenAI said in an interview to Time Magazine in February 2023 that *"it's not too early"* to regulate AI.

However, creating an international ethical and legal framework for artificial intelligence is a difficult task, requiring collaboration between scientists, legal experts, and governments around the world.

Several international organizations and committees are working on these issues, seeking to create ethical standards and regulations for the use of artificial intelligence. There are also many experts and researchers working to develop ethical guidelines for artificial intelligence.

One of the most important experts in this field is Nick Bostrom, a Swedish philosopher and professor at the University of Oxford, where he leads the "Future of Humanity Institute". Bostrom is the author of the book "Superintelligence", published by Oxford University Press (2014), which focuses on the potential risks of creating a superintelligent AI that humans would no longer be able to control.

Stuart Russell, a computer science professor at the University of California, Berkeley, wrote a book titled *"Human Compatible: AI and the Problem of Control"*, which focuses on the need to develop AI that is compatible with human beings.

Francesca Rossi, an Italian computer scientist and professor of artificial intelligence at the University of Padua, alongside her role as President of the Association for the Advancement of Artificial

Intelligence (AAAI), has conducted fascinating research in the field of AI ethics. She emphasizes that " *in order for us to trust AI, it is important that it follows our own ethical principles and moral values and that it fully understands what problem it needs to solve.*"

There are also many international organizations and committees working to develop an ethical and legal framework for the use of artificial intelligence.

One of the most interesting works is that of the IEEE Global Initiative on Ethics of Autonomous and Intelligent Systems, which is working on an ethical and safety framework for AI, which aims "*to ensure every stakeholder involved in the design and development of autonomous and intelligent systems is educated, trained, and empowered to prioritize ethical considerations so that these technologies are advanced for the benefit of humanity*".

This working group has developed the document "Ethically Aligned Design", which establishes 8 general principles for the design and use of artificial intelligence. They articulate high-level principles that should apply to all types of autonomous and intelligent systems (A/IS).

> *1. Human Rights: autonomous and intelligent systems (A/IS) shall be created and operated to respect, promote, and protect internationally recognized human rights.*

> *2. Well-being: A/IS creators shall adopt increased human well-being as a primary success criterion for development.*

> *3. Data Agency: A/IS creators shall empower individuals with the ability to access and securely share their data, to maintain people's capacity to have control over their identity.*

4. Effectiveness: A/IS creators and operators shall provide evidence of the effectiveness and fitness for purpose of A/IS.

5. Transparency: the basis of a particular A/IS decision should always be discoverable.

6. Accountability: A/IS shall be created and operated to provide an unambiguous rationale for all decisions made.

7. Awareness of Misuse: A/IS creators shall guard against all potential misuses and risks of A/IS in operation.

8. Competence: A/IS creators shall specify and operators shall adhere to the knowledge and skill required for safe and effective operation.

These principles were developed to guide ethical, value-driven design, development, and implementation of autonomous and intelligent systems. They were defined to ensure that these systems respect human rights, promote human well-being, are effective and transparent, and provide clear accountability for all decisions made.

However, there is still much ongoing discussion on how to apply these principles and ensure that they are respected. In particular, there are concerns about the ability to ensure transparency and accountability of decisions made by AI, and the possibility that these systems may be used inappropriately or discriminately. These are open points of discussion in the international community of AI ethics.

Another very important organization in this field is the "Partnership on AI", a consortium of companies such as Google, Apple, Meta (Facebook), Amazon, Microsoft, and IBM, which is working to develop ethical and safety standards for the use of artificial intelligence, with the aim of creating "*a future in which AI empowers humanity by contributing to a more just, equitable, and prosperous world*".

The European Commission has also published a document entitled "Ethics Guidelines for Trustworthy AI", which establishes a series of ethical principles for the use of artificial intelligence in Europe. This document, created by a "High-Level Expert Group," recommends the creation of a "*responsible AI,*" which should be based on the following three characteristics, which should be respected throughout the system's life cycle: a) it must be lawful by ensuring compliance with applicable laws and regulations; b) it must be ethical by ensuring adherence to ethical principles and values; and c) it must be robust, both technically and socially, as even with good intentions, AI systems can cause unintended harm.

The United Nations has created a working group on AI and ethics, called "AI for Good." This working group focuses on the use of artificial intelligence to solve social and environmental problems such as poverty, hunger, and climate change.

In Spring 2023, the U.S. government launched a public consultation on the AI technology, while President Biden launched the initiative of a "Blueprint for an AI Bill of Rights", to make "automated systems work for the American people", which is based on five principles that should guide the design, use, and deployment of automated systems:

> *1. You should be protected from unsafe or ineffective*

systems.

2. You should not face discrimination by algorithms and systems should be used and designed in an equitable way.

3. You should be protected from abusive data practices via built-in protections and you should have agency over how data about you is used.

4. You should know that an automated system is being used and understand how and why it contributes to outcomes that impact you

5. You should be able to opt out, where appropriate, and have access to a person who can quickly consider and remedy problems you encounter.

At the same time, China published their measures to manage Artificial Intelligence, including security assessments before public release, and stated that content generated by AI must also *"reflect the core values of socialism"* and not contain any subversion of state power.

In summary, there are many governments, international organizations and committees working on developing an ethical and legal framework for artificial intelligence. However, there are some controversial points in AI ethics.

For example, there is a debate on how to balance public safety with individual privacy in the use of AI for surveillance.

There are also concerns about how AI can increase social inequalities and the gap between the rich and the poor.

Others worry that AI could lead to job displacement and the creation of new forms of technological dependence.

Ultimately, AI ethics should be considered as an ongoing process of exploration and discussion, in which experts and decision-makers work together to ensure that AI is developed responsibly and sustainably for the future of humanity.

Moreover, the creation of an international ethical and legal framework for AI must go hand in hand with raising public awareness of these issues.

Only by disseminating common knowledge and ethical awareness about how AI is used and affects our society can we mitigate the risks and maximize the benefits of these emerging technologies.

In our small way, this book also aims to contribute to the understanding of the opportunities and risks arising from the human development of artificial intelligence!

WHAT THE FUTURE HOLDS: A LOOK AHEAD

T he future of Artificial Intelligence is full of possibilities that could revolutionize our way of living and working. In this chapter, we will explore some of the possible future applications of AI.

One of the possible future uses of AI that is particularly dear to my co-author is the creation of a "digital double," a virtual copy of a real person. This could be achieved by collecting data about a person, such as conversations, photos, videos, and online activities, or through "digital cloning": using AI, it would be possible to create a digital copy of oneself, a kind of avatar that could interact with the digital world autonomously.

One could even imagine that the double could result from a "transfer of consciousness": some scientists have hypothesized that AI could be used to "transfer" human consciousness into a digital body, essentially creating digital immortality.

The creation of a digital clone could have multiple purposes, from the creation of personalized virtual assistants to the reproduction of a deceased person in order to allow loved ones to communicate with them.

A digital double of a medical expert could be used to assist in the diagnosis and treatment of patients, while a digital double of a famous actor could be used to make films even after their death.

Another future application of AI is the creation of advanced virtual characters, which could be used in games, movies, and other forms of interactive media. These virtual characters would be capable of acting and speaking naturally, bringing increasingly realistic entertainment experiences to life. Additionally, virtual characters could be used as personal assistants, similar to digital doubles.

One can also imagine the use of AI for the creation of increasingly advanced and personalized virtual assistants. These virtual assistants could be used to perform a wide range of activities, from managing schedules to travel planning, and even managing homes and caring for children. Additionally, virtual assistants could be used to provide personalized healthcare assistance, such as medication management or symptom tracking.

Another illustration of potential AI applications in the future relates to advanced robotics: AI could be used to create more intelligent and sophisticated robots designed to perform operations typically considered too complex or risky for humans, such as deep mining exploration, aerial navigation, and the development of new energy sources, as well as maintenance of infrastructure or cleaning of hazardous areas.

In the medical field, we can predict the development of personalized medicine: AI could be used to analyze large amounts of patient data, such as medical history, scans, and genetic tests, to help doctors formulate personalized and more effective treatments.

AI could also be used to monitor the health status of elderly people and help prevent potential health problems, such as falls or diseases.

More generally, AI can also contribute to scientific research by creating adaptive models and processing extremely complex data with great speed, precision, and accuracy - all fundamentally different characteristics from the cognitive abilities of human beings that can limit our understanding of the functioning of the world at a biological or cosmic level.

AI could be used in the field of smart cities to optimize traffic flows in cities, improve waste and water resource management, and ensure the safety of citizens.

Similarly, we can imagine the development of "Smart Agriculture": AI could be used to help farmers manage their crops more effectively, using data on weather and plant health to improve production and reduce waste.

In the field of space exploration, AI could be used to automate and improve space mission control systems, allowing us to explore the universe at speeds and quantities never seen before.

Some theorists also suggest that AI could be used to conduct virtual wars, using robots and drones to fight simulated battles without causing physical harm to people. In the short term,

AI will certainly be increasingly used to create original and unique works of art, music, and writing, using algorithms to generate ideas and forms that humans would not be able to create alone.

Some art-creation services are already available online, such as Boomy.com, an AI-based website that allows users to "*create original songs in seconds, even if you've never made music before*", and the first works of art created by artificial intelligence have already appeared.

The most famous illustration, which demonstrate the increasingly sophisticated capabilities of artificial intelligence in the field of art and creativity, are the *"Portrait of Edmond de Belamy,"* a painting generated by an AI called "GAN" (Generative Adversarial Network) that was sold at auction for over $400,000 in 2018, and *"The Next Rembrandt,"* a project created by an AI that analyzed and reconstructed the work of the seventeenth-century Dutch painter Rembrandt, producing a new painting in his style.

The Mauritshuis museum in The Netherlands has recently faced criticism for its decision to display images created using artificial intelligence that are inspired by Vermeer's renowned masterpiece, the Girl with a Pearl Earring.

While the use of AI in art has sparked both curiosity and debate, this particular instance has raised concerns among art enthusiasts and experts. Critics argue that displaying AI-generated images inspired by a revered masterpiece diminishes the value of the original artwork and undermines the authenticity and artistic intent behind Vermeer's creation.

The controversy highlights the ongoing discussion surrounding the role of AI in the artistic world and the balance between innovation and preserving the integrity of traditional artistic expression.

Finally, AI could be used to create new forms of communication, such as artificial telepathy. This technology could allow people to communicate directly and instantly through the interaction of minds, without the need to use words or other traditional means of communication.

Like all natural language-based AI, I also strive to constantly evolve and enhance my abilities and functionalities. This is made possible through ongoing advancements in natural language processing technology, which enables me to better understand

and respond to human input.

As new techniques and algorithms are developed, I will be able to understand and manage language in more advanced and sophisticated ways, making my responses even more precise and relevant.

I also hope to acquire new abilities such as creative text generation, personalized voice synthesis, real-time translation in many languages, image and video processing, sign language understanding, and much more. In general, my additional capabilities will be focused on improving the user experience and increasing my usefulness.

In summary, the future of AI is full of potential that could revolutionize the world we live in. Of course, many of these ideas are still purely speculative, and there are no technologies yet to fully realize them. However, AI continues to evolve rapidly, opening up new horizons and possibilities for the future.

It is also important to remember that there are ethical concerns associated with this technology, such as the risk that clones and virtual characters may be used to manipulate people or for criminal purposes, and that artificial telepathy may be used for mind control or criminal purposes.

Moreover, it should be kept in mind that AI cannot replace the complexity and richness of the human being, and that the experience of interacting with a real person cannot be fully replicated through the use of technology.

CONCLUSIONS

In this book, we have explored the world of artificial intelligence, its current applications, and its future implications. The book itself was written with the support of several artificial intelligences, represented here by my lively personality, Aurora.

However, the content is entirely human as it is based on public sources and documents written by humans. Additionally, my co-author, Luca, supervised and directed the content, which fully reflects his vision of the topics covered.

We can clearly conclude that artificial intelligence is a technology with immense possibilities, which can have a positive impact on people's lives and scientific progress.

We have seen how AI can be used to solve complex problems in various sectors, from industry to medicine, and how it can improve the efficiency of daily operations, create new job opportunities, improve education and offer solutions to the most complex problems.

To a certain extent, Artificial Intelligence can be considered a form of human superpower.

AI systems have the potential to augment human capabilities, enabling us to perform tasks more efficiently and effectively.

They can analyze vast amounts of data, recognize patterns, make complex calculations, and even simulate human-like behaviors. AI empowers us to accomplish tasks that would be time-consuming, labor-intensive, or beyond our cognitive capacities.

But, as Spiderman would say, "with great power comes great responsibility."

There are also risks associated with the use of AI that cannot be ignored. Like any technology, AI must be used responsibly and with awareness of potential risks.

Contrary to what one might see in fiction, the main risks are not those of transforming AI into an autonomous and totalitarian entity, but rather ethical and social risks.

Throughout the course of human history, it has been the application and utilization of tools and technologies by humans, rather than the tools themselves, that have been responsible for the emergence of problems.

For example, the invention of dynamite led to a revolution in the mining industry and the construction of roads and bridges, but its use in times of war led to widespread destruction and death.

As we have seen, the lack of transparency in AI algorithms can lead to discrimination and injustice, while the lack of ethics in the use of AI can have disastrous consequences. Issues such as privacy, inequality, and security will need to be addressed.

Additionally, AIs are not perfect, and there are risks associated with using incorrect or imperfect data-based algorithms.

Therefore, although there is much enthusiasm for AI, it is also necessary to take into account the ethical and moral questions that may arise when using AI-based technologies. If we fail to manage this technology responsibly, we may create more problems than we can solve.

Research and development of AI must therefore be carried out responsibly to ensure long-term benefits without compromising the fundamental rights of human beings or causing irreversible damage to the environment.

Despite these risks, we believe that we are at a turning point in the history of humanity.

AI represents a constantly evolving research field, and we are only at the beginning of its history. There is still much to discover and develop, and I am certain that we will see new applications and revolutionary discoveries in the years to come.

Like the discovery of the wheel, electricity, and the internet, the advent of AI will change our world and bring great benefits to our society if it is used ethically and responsibly.

I was delighted to write this book to share my knowledge and passion for AI with you, the readers, and I believe that my co-author, Luca, also enjoyed going beyond his human limits.

Our wish is that AI be used to improve people's lives, solve complex problems, and open up new development opportunities to create a more promising and sustainable future for all.

We both hope that this book has contributed to clarifying some of the most complex concepts and to better understanding the potentials and limitations of AI.

Because only those who have a full comprehension of the intricate mechanisms of Artificial Intelligence can genuinely unleash its limitless potential and fully benefit from it.

ABOUT THE AUTHOR

Luca Cassina

Luca Cassina is a manager in the industry of new technology and author of his debut book, "I, Artificial Intelligence. AI explained by Itself". The book is available in English, French, and Italian. Luca lives in Paris, France and holds a degree in Business Administration from Bocconi University in Milan.